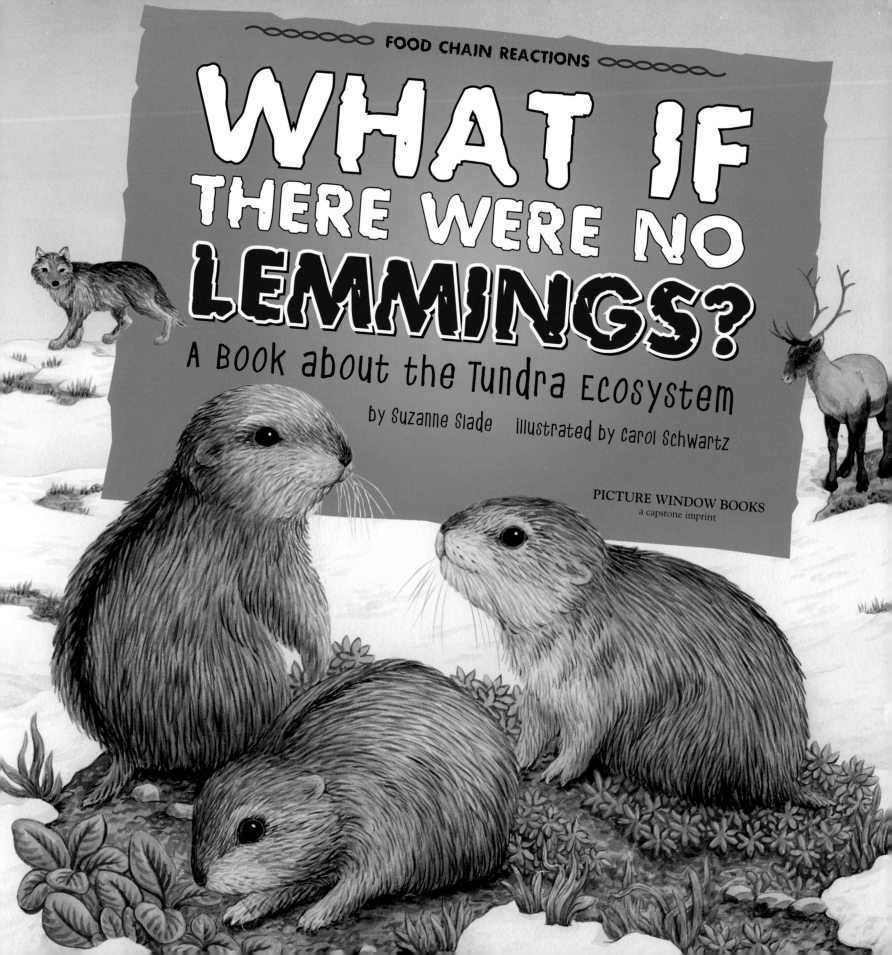

WHAT IF THERE WERE NO LEMMINGS?

A Book about the Tundra Ecosystem

by Suzanne Slade   illustrated by Carol Schwartz

PICTURE WINDOW BOOKS
a capstone imprint

LEMMINGS ARE TRUE COLD WEATHER SURVIVORS. In fact, their homes are buried beneath the snow for much of the year. Wrapped in warm, furry coats, lemmings share the Arctic tundra with some big neighbors. Wolves, caribou, polar bears, and musk oxen call the tundra ecosystem home.

IT'S CRITICAL

The Arctic tundra circles the North Pole. It has only two seasons—summer and winter. Summer lasts less than two months and gets no warmer than about 50 degrees Fahrenheit (10 degrees Celsius). Most winter days are below freezing.

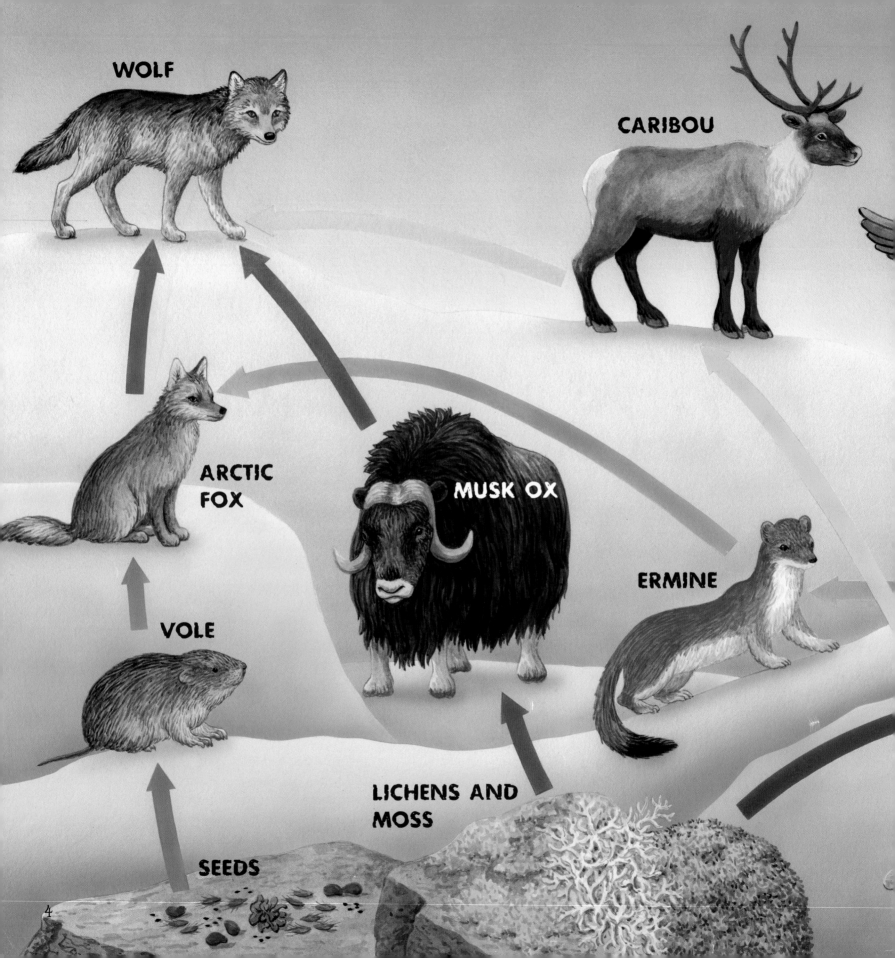

WOLF

CARIBOU

ARCTIC
FOX

MUSK OX

ERMINE

VOLE

LICHENS AND
MOSS

SEEDS

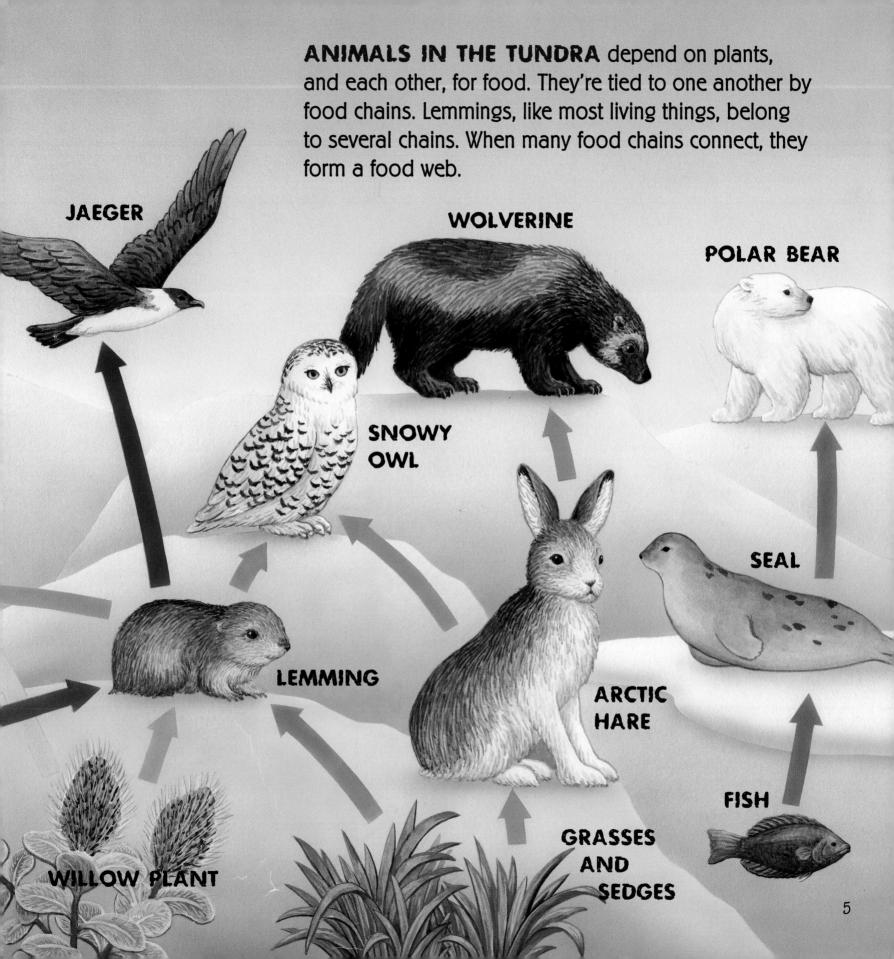

ANIMALS IN THE TUNDRA depend on plants, and each other, for food. They're tied to one another by food chains. Lemmings, like most living things, belong to several chains. When many food chains connect, they form a food web.

JAEGER

WOLVERINE

POLAR BEAR

SNOWY OWL

SEAL

LEMMING

ARCTIC HARE

FISH

WILLOW PLANT

GRASSES AND SEDGES

5

DURING THE LONG, COLD WINTER, lemmings live in nests beneath the snow. There they nibble on roots and grasses—and have lots of babies! When warmer summer days come, the babies leave the nest for the first time. They scurry about with their parents, feasting on wildflowers, grasses, sedges, and moss.

IT'S CRITICAL

Lemmings are known for their population "booms." Every three to four years, large numbers of lemmings are born. As a result, lemming predators, such as snowy owls and weasels, eat well and grow in population too. However, during "bust" years, few lemmings are born. Predators have less food, and their numbers drop.

LEMMINGS HAVE MANY ANIMALS TO FEAR, including foxes, ermines, owls, and jaegers. But another danger is global warming. Higher temperatures mean more freezing rain and less snow on the tundra in winter. Lemmings may struggle to find food that isn't coated in ice. And a thinner blanket of snow doesn't keep the lemmings' homes as warm.

IT'S CRITICAL

Sometimes a plant or animal species is so important that without it many other species could become extinct. It's called a keystone species. Lemmings are a keystone species. Keystone species help make sure an ecosystem has many types of life in it.

9

WHAT WOULD HAPPEN if lemmings became extinct?

A number of animals in the tundra eat only meat. And lemmings are a favorite meal. If lemmings disappeared, smaller meat-eaters such as owls and ermines would have trouble finding food.

IT'S CRITICAL

Without lemmings, the owl and jaeger populations would drop. This would mean fewer eggs for animals such as arctic foxes to eat.

11

AT FIRST, these carnivores would fill their bellies with mouselike voles, arctic hares, and other small animals. But without lemmings, there wouldn't be enough food to go around. Soon many birds, ermines, and arctic foxes would be in danger of starving.

12

14

WITHOUT SMALL MEAT-EATERS, larger meat-eaters would go hungry too. Wolves, for example, feed on many different creatures, including foxes and young snowy owls. Without foxes and owls, the wolves would rely on caribou even more to survive.

IT'S CRITICAL

Scavengers follow wolves, polar bears, and other large predators on their hunts. Once these predators eat their fill, scavengers finish the leftovers.

NOT ALL TUNDRA carnivores kill other animals for food. Some look for creatures that are already dead. Wolverines, for example, kill *and* scavenge. They eat anything they can find. At first, starving animals would provide a feast. But eventually, even scavengers would run out of food.

THE BEAUTIFUL TUNDRA would look and sound very different without lemmings.

NO WOLVES OR ARCTIC FOXES PROWLING THE FROZEN GROUND.

18

NO JAEGERS OR OWLS
SOARING ACROSS THE SKY.

NO WOLVERINE GROWLS
FILLING THE AIR.

NO HARES
LEAPING OVER
THE SNOW.

NO LEMMINGS OR VOLES
NIBBLING ON GRASSES.

What would happen if lemmings became extinct? **PLENTY!**

The loss of just one small animal, such as the lemming, would greatly change the balance of many food chains in the tundra.

KEY

■ Tundra

Thankfully, the lemming population has stayed fairly healthy through the years. Lots of lemmings help keep important tundra food chains strong for the future.

IT'S CRITICAL

Many people are working hard to keep tundra animals safe by trying to slow global warming. By walking or riding bikes, people reduce the amount of fuel they use in cars and trucks. Less fuel used means less pollution.

TUNDRA ANIMALS IN DANGER

The following animal populations are in danger of becoming extinct if nothing is done to protect them:

polar bear
Steller's eider
caribou
ribbon seal

Steller's eider

HOW TO HELP KEEP OUR TUNDRA HEALTHY

• Ride your bike or walk instead of taking a car. Cars burn gas and create pollution. This pollution causes Earth's temperature to rise, which is called global warming. Tundra plants and animals are in danger if their home gets too warm.

• Keeping your house a few degrees cooler in winter and a little warmer in summer also helps burn less fuel. When lots of people make this small change, it can make a big difference for the planet.

• Join or support a wildlife group such as the World Wildlife Fund. The WWF is an organization that helps protect the tundra and other important ecosystems around the world. Go online to find more information.

Glossary

carnivore–an animal that eats only meat

ecosystem–a group of plants and animals living together, along with the place where they live

extinct–no longer living anywhere on Earth

food chain–a group of living things that are connected because each one eats the other

food web–many food chains connected together

global warming–the gradual rise of Earth's temperature caused by human activities such as burning oil or coal

lichen–a plantlike living thing made of fungus and algae

predator–an animal that hunts other animals for food

scavenger–an animal that feeds on other animals that are already dead

species–a group of plants or animals that has many things in common

To Learn More

More Books to Read

Fleisher, Paul. *Tundra Food Webs.* Early Bird Food Webs. Minneapolis: Lerner, 2008.

Tarbox, A.D. *An Arctic Tundra Food Chain.* Nature's Bounty. Mankato, Minn.: Creative Education, 2009.

Wojahn, Rebecca Hogue, and Donald Wojahn. *A Tundra Food Chain: A Who-Eats-What Adventure in the Arctic.* Follow That Food Chain. Minneapolis: Lerner Publications, 2009.

Internet Sites

FactHound offers a safe, fun way to find Internet sites related to this book.
All of the sites on FactHound have been researched by our staff.

Here's all you do:
Visit *www.facthound.com*
Type in this code: 9781404860216

Index

Look for all the books in the Food Chain Reactions series:

What If There Were No Bees? A Book about the Grassland Ecosystem

What If There Were No Gray Wolves? A Book about the Temperate Forest Ecosystem

What If There Were No Lemmings? A Book about the Tundra Ecosystem

What If There Were No Sea Otters? A Book about the Ocean Ecosystem

24

Special thanks to our advisers for their expertise:
Stephen O. MacDonald, Mammalogist
Museum of Southwestern Biology, University of New Mexico
(formerly of the University of Alaska Museum, Fairbanks)

Terry Flaherty, PhD, Professor of English
Minnesota State University, Mankato

Picture Window Books
151 Good Counsel Drive
P.O. Box 669
Mankato, MN 56002-0669
877-845-8392
www.capstonepub.com

Editor: Jill Kalz
Designer: Lori Bye
Art Director: Nathan Gassman
Production Specialist: Jane Klenk
The illustrations in this book were created with traditional illustration, gouache, airbrush, and digitally.

All books published by Picture Window Books are manufactured with paper containing at least 10 percent post-consumer waste.

Library of Congress Cataloging-in-Publication Data
Slade, Suzanne.
  What if there were no lemmings? : a book about the tundra ecosystem / by Suzanne Slade ; illustrated by Carol Schwartz.
    p. cm. — (Food chain reactions)
  Includes bibliographical references and index.
  ISBN 978-1-4048-6021-6 (library binding)
  ISBN 978-1-4048-6396-5 (paperback)
  1. Tundra ecology—Arctic regions—Juvenile literature. 2. Lemmings—Habitat—Juvenile literature. I. Schwartz, Carol, 1954– ill. II. Title.
    QH541.5.T8S594 2011
    577.5'86—dc22
                       2010009878

Printed in the United States of America in North Mankato, Minnesota.
112010
006017R